Palm Beach
Fashion Secrets and More

Anita Gabler

Cover: "AL FRESCO", acrylic on canvas, 40" X 48", artist Roy Fairchild - Woodard, Surrey, England

Palm Beach Fashion Secrets And More

Copyright © 2017 Anita Gabler

Revised 2018

All rights reserved.

First Edition

Book Design by Pamela Boullier Ross

Set in Book Antiqua

All rights reserved including the right of reproduction in whole or in part in any form by any means, electronic, multimedia, or mechanical, including photocopying, recording or by any information storage and/or retrieval syste, without the prior written permission of the author, Anita Gabler.

Library of Congress Cataloging-in Publication Data

Gabler, Anita

Palm Beach Fashion Secrets and More / Anita Gabler

ISBN 978-0-615-55060-2

> "... a girl should be two things, classy and fabulous."
> ~ *Coco Chanel*

acknowledgements

Thank you to my family, friends and fashion experts who have inspired me to write this book. I would especially like to thank my husband Jim for his endless support and editing, my daughter Tricia for her suggestions and support, my grandson E. J. for his computer expertise, my sister Patty Holloway for her fashion suggestions, my dearest high school friend Eileen Huston for her editing and encouragement, Pamela Boullier Ross for her artistic talents in designing this publication and my editor Ellen Boland for adding perfection to my written word. Without all of you this book would never have become a reality. I thank you from the bottom of my heart!

PALM BEACH FASHION SECRETS & MORE

To Nina
My beautiful mother

contents

Introduction

Chapter 1   page 3
Palm Beach Fashion
- Explore
- Putting Your Wardrobe Together
- Chic Accessories
- Closet Organization
- Wardrobe Essentials
- Daytime to Evening Looks
- Packing for a Ten Day Trip all in a Carry-on Suitcase

Chapter 2   page 29
Naked Secrets
- Exercise Essential
- Total Make Over Program Testimony
- Skin Care
- Make Up
- Beauty Accessories/Products

Chapter 3   page 41
Island Shopping Secrets
- Department Stores
- Designer Boutiques
- Speciality Shops

contents

Chapter 4   page 53

Fashionable Dining Experiences & Secrets

- American
- Asian
- French
- Italian
- Seafood
- Small Plates
- Steak Houses
- Carry Out

Chapter 5   page 65

Chic Island Hotels & Secrets

- The Bradley Park Hotel
- Brazilian Court
- Breakers
- Chesterfield
- Colony Palm Beach
- Palm Beach Historic Inn
- Four Seasons

Summary   page 69

Secrets & Pleasures

- Tips for a New "Palm Beach" You
- Favorite & Guilty Pleasures

Via on Worth Avenue, Palm Beach, Florida

introduction

When visitors ask me how I like living on the Island of Palm Beach, I respond with, "Who wouldn't want to live in paradise?" With a sky and ocean in beautiful shades of blue, a landscape dotted with majestic palm trees and lawns manicured to perfection, the island has the feel of a Renoir painting. There is a formal informality about the residents who are friendly, polite and well dressed. Rarely, if ever, will you see a native wearing cutoffs or blue jeans. Most Palm Beachers dress up for dinner and by that I mean, at a minimum, an upscale casual look. The year-round perfect weather provides ample opportunities for dining al fresco with friends, enjoying a day at the beach and swimming in the ocean. Sporting activities are readily available twelve months of the year. Biking, walking, tennis, boating and golf abound for the outdoors type, musical performances and educational lectures at The Society of the Four Arts and Campus on the Lake entertain the more culturally minded and for those who want mental stimulation a bridge game is always available.

Shopping is a major pastime for both Palm Beach natives and visitors with the exclusive Worth Avenue, its surrounding vias and other nearby Island shops offering the finest in clothing, jewelry, art and accessories.

I have always had a passion for fashion and can't help but enjoy sharing that with others. For the past seven years I have hosted fashion luncheons on the Island featuring professionals sharing their expertise from clothing, perfume and accessory designers to authors and photographers. These fashionable get togethers introduce the latest and greatest on-trend and fashion-forward styles of Worth Avenue and the surrounding Island shops. When it comes to one-stop glamorous shopping, Palm Beach has it all. Not so readily available are its coveted fashion secrets, secrets I am about to share with you.

Fashion design by Susan E. Riley

1
Palm Beach Fashion

Colorful clothing is paramount in Palm Beach. Having relocated from the northeast, I quickly realized my dark and neutral wardrobe of mostly heavy fabrics needed some changes. As I explored the Island's shops I was mesmerized by the richness of colors, materials and styles. The famous fashion designer Coco Chanel said, "a girl should be two things: classy and fabulous" and that is the epitome of Palm Beach fashion. From a stylish, colorful and casual look during the day to upscale casual or formal dress at night, I have embraced Palm Beach fashion. Now the fun begins. Let me share my secrets to creating that fabulous Palm Beach look.

First of all, have fun with fashion! Shopping should be an exploration. It is a chance to express who you are or who you want to be. Venture into the unknown and try new styles, colors and trends while always looking fashionably put together. Make shopping an exciting adventure and who knows where you will find something.

Shopping for unique designer pieces is the foundation of fashion and finding unexpected fabulous pieces in boutiques is always a thrill in itself. Imagine walking along Worth Avenue and seeing a purse, like the one pictured here, in a store window that you absolutely adore.

Buy it! This floral Gucci purse will never go out of style. It's a piece of art. The quality and Italian craftsmanship of the antique silver toned hardware, tiger head closure, hand painted edges, three

separate interior compartments and hand stitched details are superb. The iconic Gucci Blooms print is a fabulous fashion piece. Now all you need is clothing that will look great with it, new or right out of your existing wardrobe. This purse will become a staple in your closet never going out of style, a great investment.

putting your wardrobe together

Vintage couture clothing shops are also great places to peruse, often with more competitive prices. In the photo below, the Chanel top and pearls were found at Fashionista Palm Beach, a vintage couture consignment shop. The vintage Chanel car wash skirt (a skirt cut in strips resembling the strips swishing around in an automatic car wash) was purchased from 1st Dibbs online

consignment shop. Of course Saks Fifth Avenue on Worth Avenue is always full of great finds like these Louboutin ballet flats.

MIX couture pieces with less expensive ones while always seeking chic and it will be hard to detect the luxury pieces from the less expensive ones. Be careful that your outfits are not matchy-matchy as that can be boring. Have fun and be creative and your look will be more interesting. Buy individual pieces that you especially like to go with several looks. Mix a designer handbag or clutch with a cashmere summer weight sweater or tunic top, straight leg slacks and ballet flats or wedge sandals and you are ready for just about anything.

MINIMIZE THE BLING. Too much bling can overwhelm a

look. Accent your outfit with a statement pair of earrings or a bold necklace. You can achieve a chic Island look by mixing quality faux jewelry with real and not have to spend a fortune. Just don't overdo it!

LOOK GOOD. FEEL GOOD. Clothing should always be comfortable. Know what suits you and your confidence will shine through. Know what flatters your body type. For example, if your waist is thick or if you are short-waisted, choose a shift or drop-waisted dress. To assess your body shape, go to the website www.shopyourshape.com and click on the tab, Body Shape Guide. It will help you determine what styles are best for your figure.

KNOW YOUR COLORS. If you are not sure which colors suit you best, go to www.coloranalysis.com and take a free online color analysis test. The test determines colors that best complements you based on your natural coloring.

If your skin has blue undertones (usually brunette, black and blond hair) then wear bright colors such as sapphire blue, navy, fuchsia and soft shades such as mint green, soft yellow and coral. If your skin has yellow undertones (usually redheads and strawberry blonds) then autumn and spring colors look best. Try rust, copper, butterscotch and various shades of brown.

Debating on whether to buy something or not? Photos are more telling than the mirror. Take a picture of the front, back and side views.

THEN MAKE A MENTAL CHECKLIST.

✓ How do I look and feel in this outfit?
✓ Is the fabric comfortable?
✓ Does the style flatter my body type?
✓ Is anything too tight or loose?
✓ Does it need alterations?
✓ Are the colors right for my skin tone?
✓ Am I buying this just because it is on sale?

Be honest with yourself! If it doesn't look fabulous on you, don't buy it leaving it to hang in the back of your closet.

I highly recommend the book, *What to Wear for the Rest of Your Life* by Kim Johnson Gross. Kim was a guest speaker at one of my Women and Fashion luncheons. She offers calming fashion advice about how to choose clothes that show off your shape and style. Kim's engaging stories will help you evolve gracefully from businesswoman, wife and/or mother to empty-nester and globe-trotting adventurer. In any role, your outfit portrays your outer look and your style expresses your inner beauty.

A little edginess is always fun and can be achieved by mixing different colors and fabrics. Utilize your best colors and don't be afraid of mixing them. For example, red with chartreuse (greenish/yellow) creates an incredible combination. Flame orange looks fabulous with olive or cobalt blue and navy with white is always refreshing. Mix leather tops with a zebra clutch, jean jackets with a colorful fun skirt, wide belts with a pencil skirt and sandals decorated with colorful stones. Don a fedora or boater hat with wide leg pants and a fitted top, narrow leg pants with a loose fitting top and add beautiful scarves tied in stylish ways, oversized sunglasses and pearl necklaces. Fashion evolves. Be the one to set a trend.

chic accessories

Always choose a fabulous accessory for your final look but keep in mind my simple rule: Understated Elegance with an Edge is the secret to looking sensational everyday!

Shopping for accessories. Regardless of your body shape, accessories are important. They can completely change the look of a day or evening outfit. Without them you risk looking boring! Just remember to not over do it.

BAGS

A tote is essential for travel and shopping and safest with a zipper closure. Before you buy it, make sure your basics (cosmetic bag, wallet, hairbrush, phone, travel umbrella) fit.

This Celine bag with zipper closure and pockets for phone and other accessories is one of my favorites. Tory Burch's leaf

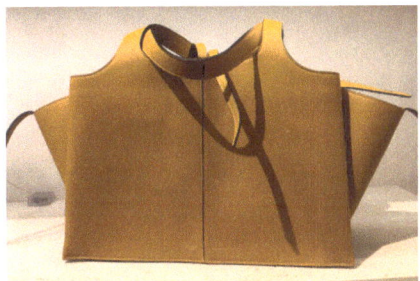 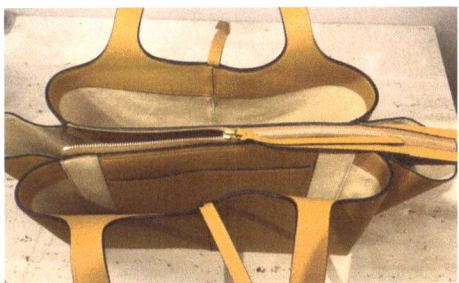

applique straw tote keeps you chic while holding all you need shopping at local green markets, lounging at the beach or exploring on a weekend getaway. A clutch is the perfect evening accessory and a bright color is a great Palm Beach look. Mildred Hoit in Palm Beach is my go-to for wonderful clutches and other styles of bags made in Italy.

A shoulder bag, or two, in a neutral color is an everyday necessary staple. I love this medium size tote by Michael Kors (right) and the straw tote bag by Tory Burch (left).

"The joy of dressing is an art."
~ John Galliano

SHOES

What you put on your feet builds the foundation for a complete look. Marilyn Monroe once said, "Give a girl the right shoe and she can conquer the world." A print flat or animal skin beautifully accents a solid color outfit. It is easy to be safe but super fun to go bold.

Go to **Jimmy Choo** located at 254 Worth Avenue (561-655-3635) for glamorous heels with a "playfully daring spirit." Jimmy Choo opened his first store in London on Motcomb Street. He did something right as now there are over 167 stores in 35 countries.

Sandals are a must-have item in Palm Beach with stores all over the Island carrying unusual designs. Put your creativity to work and choose the leather, style and embellishments. It is a perfect solution to getting exactly what you want.

These two stores are amazing for custom sandals:

Francesco Pasta, 34 Via Capri, 323 Worth Avenue (561-659-6909)

Il Sandalo, 240 Worth Avenue (561-805-8674)

Ballet flats are a must-have for comfortable walking shoes. Look for bold and metallic colors to make a statement with basic slacks and skirts.

For endless selections of ballet flats, try these two shoe shops on Worth Avenue:

Pretty Ballerinas, 150 Worth Avenue (561-659-6670) and

Cashmere Beach, via Bici, 313 1/2 Worth Avenue (561-802-3300)

Walk down Worth Avenue and you will see someone wearing Needle Point slippers by **Stubbs & Wootton**. Check this Palm Beach classic store at 340 Worth Avenue (561-655-6857). Percy Steinhart, founder and owner, was a guest speaker at one of my fashion luncheons and he stated, "I saw something happening in Palm Beach, all of my friends were wearing these velvet evening slippers."

Steinhart found a factory in Spain to make his quirky velvet slippers with emblems ranging from harlequins to crests and even skulls! In 1993 Stubbs & Wootton was born adding needlepoint designs to the velvet slippers. He even made a pair of red slippers for a Pope.

You will be comfortable in them day into evening, with jeans and dinner clothes and can have them monogrammed for special occasions. You'll also see them up north with stores in New York City and the Hamptons.

JEWELRY

Sequin, 330 S County Road (561-833-7300) and 219 Worth Avenue (561-328-8406) are my favorite luxury costume jewelry stores on the Island. Founded by two sisters Kim Dryer and Linda Awe in the year 2000, they describe their jewelry as "contemporary chic with a romantic edge, known for distinctive, directional jewelry that transcends fast fashion." 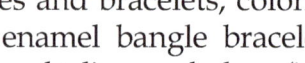With vintage inspired pieces, bridal collections, color karma necklaces and bracelets, colorful enamel bangle bracelets and talisman chokers (just to name a few), you can create your individual style statement.

Mildred Hoit, 265 Sunrise Avenue (561-833-6010) has a great selection of costume and semi-precious jewelry. Clara Williams Company, responsible for their incredible designs, is known for magnetic ends that allow you to mix, match, add to and change the look of any necklace, bracelet, earring or ring. An added bonus, their gift wrapping is exceptional!

Tiffany & Co., 259 Worth Avenue (561-659-6090) represents many beautiful designers. Two well-known talented designers for sleek and classy designs are Elsa Peretti and Paloma Picasso. My favorites are Elsa's bone cuff bracelet in sterling silver and Paloma's gold olive leaf cuff bracelet and knot bracelet in leather and sterling.

WATCHES

A large watch is a statement piece and how nice to be able to easily see the time. Changing wristbands allows you the versatility to wear it day or night. An example is the Apple Watch. It's attractive, functional, the face is large enough to read and you can change the band to go with almost any outfit.

From being a phone, calendar and camera to having the ability to check email and text messages and have different decorative faces, it is the total arm accessory.

PINS

Vintage pins and silk flowers are great accessories. Be creative and wear one at the waist, accent your dress or top and decorate your evening purse or clutch. Have fun hunting for such adornments at vintage and resale stores.

"Style is a way to say who you are without having to speak."
~ *Rachel Zoe*

BELTS

The right belt for your body type makes you look slimmer, highlights your curves and adds style. It is an easy accessory to make an outfit pop.

My "Nina" belt above in black accents a simple houndstooth pencil skirt, the white belt completes a polka dot skirt look and the copper belt tied in a knot finishes off the matching copper pencil skirt.

My fashion company, Natalia Baldi, designed this belt. I saw a need for a wide belt without hardware that could be tied several ways. It is a poly spandex blend faux leather and comes in white, red, black, copper and navy blue. One size fits most. You can personalize my belts with your initials or other designs monogrammed on them. To order this belt email me, Anita Gabler, anitagabler@womenandfashion.net.

HATS

Fedora or Panama styles create an air of elegance and their wide brims serve as sun protectors too. Neutral hats work with everything but don't be shy of colorful statement hats to coordinate with your outfits too.

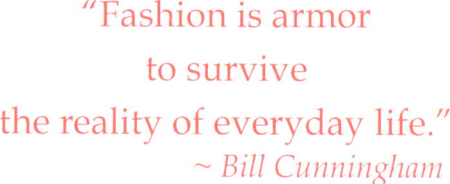

"Fashion is armor to survive the reality of everyday life."
~ Bill Cunningham

SCARVES

Hermès, 340 Royal Poinciana Way, Suite 301, (561-514-0288) has silk scarves that are works of art. The company began making silk scarves in 1937. Artists are hired to design each scarf

individually and many are signed. The designs range anywhere from the traditional horse motif to whimsical illustrations. One scarf takes 18 months to complete.

The hems are hand rolled in the Hermès factory in Lyons, France. With so many ways to wear them - halter tops, bolero jackets, wrap skirts and belts, you can add them to just about any outfit. Download the app Hermès Silk Knots on your iPhone or iPad for detailed instructions on ways to tie these magnificent scarves.

PAREOS, STOLES OR SOMETHING LILLY

In terrific colors or prints these masterpieces look fabulous worn as a skirt over a bathing suit or casually draped over the shoulder as a stole.

Who doesn't love a classic trademark Lilly? A Lilly Pulitzer colorful shift dress, made famous by Lilly herself in the 1960's, is always a Palm Beach favorite casual chic look.

You can find Lilly fashion at the **Palm Beach Lilly** stores at **The Breakers**, One South County Road (561-653-6360) and **C. Orrico**, 336 S County Road (561-659-1284)

SUNGLASSES

An oversized frame in black or tortoise shell, aviator or round creates a chic look. But remember your face shape is most important, so try different styles and see what best suits you. Take photos of yourself in different styles and study which is best for you.

organize your closet

Do you really love and wear everything in your closet? To find out, take every piece out and try them on. If you do not like how you look or feel in a particular item or haven't worn it in ages, give it away. If it is an expensive designer piece take it to a consignment shop. Use these Real Simple Slimline Flocked hangers (great space savers and they hold your clothes securely) for a neat and organized look. Order on Amazon.com. Put all selected pieces back in your closet in an orderly fashion by color and type - white blouses followed by cream, pastel and dark. Do the same for slacks, dresses, skirts and shoes.

Try your shoes on. If they hurt or you cannot walk in them because the heel is too high give them away or take them to a consignment shop. Painful pumps will ruin an evening. It's amazing how easy it is to get dressed when you have a well organized closet!

SECRET - to make your closet smell fresh try Dr. Vranjes diffuser from Florence, Italy. The Lavanda Timo (lavender and thyme) scent is devine.

*"I like my money right where I can see it
- hanging in my closet."*
~ Carrie Bradshaw

wardrobe essentials

Wardrobe essentials are important! Here are some basic Palm Beach pieces that serve as a core for multiple looks.

- ✓ Straight leg slacks in navy, white, black and ecru
- ✓ Wide leg pants
- ✓ Skirts in different styles such as pencil or A-line, solid and color patterns
- ✓ Slip, sundress and cocktail dresses
- ✓ Cashmere long cardigan sweaters
- ✓ Crisp white, ecru, stripe and colorful blouses in different styles and tops and tees

Black, navy and white tank tops, silk underpinnings, stripe and solid cotton tees (white is a must) and tunic tops in tropical fabrics such as aztec patterned or beaded

An absolute must in your wardrobe is a little black dress. In 1926, Coco Chanel introduced the black dress as a stylish and glamorous fashion. Before then, black was worn only by those in mourning or by domestic help. It's popularity has been maintained through the decades and it is here to stay. Black is versatile, slimming and comes in many styles to appeal to many women.

Dresses by La Petite di Chiara Boni (polyester elastane) are awesome! Both Neiman Marcus and Saks Fifth Avenue carry this designer. In addition to black there are many colors and styles from which to choose. Each machine-washable dress is made in Italy from raw-edge, wrinkle-free jersey.

UNDERGARMENTS!

Sometimes it's what you put on first that makes you feel fabulous. Invest time and money in buying the proper lingerie. Know your correct bra size. Our bodies change so it is a good idea to check for correct fit once in a while. Sagging bust and visible panty lines are not attractive.

Always keep strapless bras, thongs, spanks and other shaping undergarments in your wardrobe. I especially like the firm control waist cincher made by TC. It really gives your torso a nice sleek shape and it is comfortable.

"The dress must follow the body of the woman, not the body following the shape of the dress."

~ *Hubert de Givenchy*

sensational palm beach looks

#1 Pool Party

LOOK - *unassuming sexy* - bathing suit (Shan), Caftan (Emilio Pucci), flat sandals (Tory Burch), tote (C J Laing), sun hat (Eugenia Kim) and large sunglasses (Gucci). Keep in mind that a black bathing suit is the most flattering! It makes you look slimmer and tends to cover up flaws.

#2 Casual Shopping with Friends

LOOK - *casual chic* - skinny pants (Akris), tunic top (Tory Burch), sandals (Tory Burch), earrings and cuff bracelet (Stephanie Kantis) and Signature Hobo Bag (Gucci).

#3 Dinner Al Fresco

LOOK - *evening chic -* party dress (Dolce & Gabbana), high sandals (Louboutin), earrings (Stephanie Kantis), ring (David Yurman) and clutch (Jimmy Choo).

#4 Cocktail Party

LOOK - *understated elegance -* black cocktail dress (Chiara Boni), slingback pumps (Manolo Blahnik), pearl necklaces (Mikimoto), earrings (Anzie), clutch (Edie Parker) and scarf (Hèrmes).

packing for a ten day trip all in a carry-on suitcase

Packing for a trip can be exhausting, yet can be made effortless by following these simple guidelines. Basic packing items are: lightweight carry-on suitcase, tote, shoe mitts and medium packing envelope called Pack-It Specter Garment Folder made by *Eagle Creek* (www.eaglecreek.com).

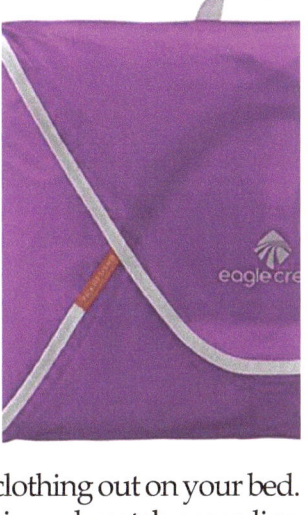

The Pack-it-Specter Garment Folder comes with a template and instructions on how to perfectly fold your clothes to fit the envelope.

Choose basic Palm Beach essential clothing and chic accessories listed previously as a guide. Keep in mind the accessories can make the outfit! In addition, you will need night gowns or pajamas, undergarments, travel umbrella and toiletries. Lay all pieces of clothing out on your bed.

Then start to mix and match according to your daily itinerary. Try to use every piece at least three times.

Make a list of the outfits and take photographs as a reference when getting dressed. For example, learn how to use this Travel Wardrobe for a sample September Tuscany Trip.

Suitcase and tote - *Gucci*, 172 Worth Avenue (561-833-6001)

Fold the 12 pieces below inside the Pack-It Garment Folder.

TRAVELLING OUTFIT ON AIRPLANE

- ✓ Tote - (pack pashmina and cashmere sweater in tote)
- ✓ Long sleeve cotton tee
- ✓ Slacks or leggings
- ✓ Wide belt
- ✓ Walking shoes
- ✓ Hat

TRAVEL ACCESSORIES

- ✓ Hi-heel & flat sandals/ballet flats (pack in shoe mitts in suitcase)
- ✓ Clutch (pack in suitcase)
- ✓ Pearls/necklace/earrings (pack in clutch)
- ✓ Extra large colorful scarf / pareo / underwear / sleepwear (pack in garment folder in suitcase)
- ✓ Toiletries & travel documents (pack in tote)

Basically you create 20 outfits out of 12 pieces of clothing and no two are alike. This does not include undergarments, 3 pairs of shoes, belt, scarf, pareo, pearls or other travel jewelry, clutch, sunhat, tote and toiletries.

For your airplane travel outfit, carry or wear the cashmere sweater, long sleeve cotton tee and stretch leggings or other comfortable pants. I like to keep a pashmina in my tote for extra warmth. Wear comfortable walking shoes such as driving loafers or espadrilles.

> "He who would travel happily
> must travel light."
> ~ *Antoine de St. Exupery*

travel wardrobe for september tuscany trip

Pool and dining terrace at Casali di Bibbiano

Arrive in Rome and travel through the Tuscan hills to the villa - Casali di Bibbiano.

DAY 1:
Upon arrival relax with a glass of wine by the pool and enjoy casual evening dinner at the villa.

 am: Bathing suit with coverup, flat sandals, sunhat, tote
pm: Ecru slacks, tank top, cashmere sweater, ballet flats, clutch

"The world is a book and those who do not travel read only one page."

~ *Saint Augustine*

DAY 2:
Explore medieval village of Montalcino and enjoy wine along the way. Romantic dinner on the villa terrace.

am: Black slacks, stripe tee, walking shoes, sunhat, tote
pm: Slip dress, pearl necklace, high sandals, clutch

Wines and Wine Shop in Montalcino

DAY 3:
Travel the lush landscapes of Tuscany to the ancient city of Siena. Dinner at the villa.

am: Skirt, white blouse, necklace, ballet flats, tote
pm: Ecru slacks, tank top, pashmina, wide belt, ballet flats

Bagno Vignoni

DAY 4:
Relax by pool and enjoy villa cooking class. Dinner in town of Bagno Vignoni.

am: Bathing suit with pareo, sunhat, flat sandals, tote
pm: Skirt, tank top, pearls, sweater, sandals

Ramparts of Florence

DAY 5:
Travel to Florence - city of art, birthplace of the Renaissance. Visit the ramparts of Florence. Dinner at the villa.

    am: Ecru slacks, print top, cashmere sweater, walking shoes, hat, tote
    pm: Slip dress, pashmina, high sandals, clutch

DAY 6:
Visit towns Pienza and Montepulciano, stop for a wine and cheese tasting. Dinner at the villa.

    am: Black slacks, white blouse, flat sandals or walking shoes, hat, tote
    pm: Slip dress, high sandals, earrings

Pienza

DAY 7:
Motor through the Umbrian hills, tour Basillica of St Francis - Assisi. Lunch at Trasimeno. Dinner at the villa.

am: Leggings, tunic top, flat sandals, sun hat, tote
pm: Skirt, tank top, wide belt, pashmina, high sandals, clutch

Castiglione della Pescaia

DAY 8:
Spend the day at Castiglione della Pescaia, a beautiful beach on the western shore of Tuscany and dine on a seafood lunch on the beach. Dinner at the villa.

am: Tunic, bathing suit, leggings, flat sandals, sun hat, tote
pm: Slip dress, pearls, cashmere sweater, high sandals, clutch

> "Wherever you go, go with all your heart."
> ~ *Confucius*

DAY 9:
Visit town of San Gimignao and Volterra. Dinner at the villa.

am: Skirt, black top, flat sandals, cashmere sweater, tote

pm: Black slacks, scarf as halter, ballet flats, clutch

San Gimignao

DAY 10:
Relax at the villa, visit a nearby spa. Farewell dinner at the villa.

am: Bathing suit with pareo, sunhat, flat sandals, tote
pm: Ecru slacks, white blouse, wide belt, ballet flats, clutch

Alberto Guadagnini, Casali di Bibbiano

"I love places that have incredble history. I love the Italian way of life. I love food. I love people. I love the attitudes of Italians."

~ Elton John

Special Note: For more information about Casali Di Bibbiano visit: www.destinationcasali.com. One of my very special secrets!

Terrace overlooking Tuscan Hills, Casali di Bibbiano

Wine Cellar, Casali di Bibbiano

Chef Massimiliano conducting cooking classes at Casali di Bibbiano

Reina, Anita and Judith at the "New You" Women and Fashion luncheon January 12, 2016 Colony Hotel, Palm Beach

2

Naked Secrets

∽

Women are beautiful inside with many wonderful talents that they share with others including chairing a charity event, volunteering for a needy cause or helping their husband, children, grandchildren and friends. Compassionate, thoughtful, kind and intelligent are some of the qualities that make a woman beautiful. This inner beauty can radiate stronger just by paying attention to some simple beauty suggestions for body, skin, makeup and hair.

exercise

Exercise is essential for keeping you healthy, your body in shape, your mind sharp and your balance strong. Exercise on a regular basis. Working out at a gym is one sure form of exercise and trainers are great motivators and help avoid injuries. I particularly enjoy tennis and biking.

Palm Beach Fitness located at 165 Chilean Avenue is an excellent gym offering free weights, Nautilus resistance, Cybex, Precor, Concept 2 and Cardio Vision. The owner/personal trainer Craig Campbell and personal trainers Mike White, Will Paul Ancheta, Mike Zingaro, Sabrina White and Nicole Edelstein are outstanding in their fields and are available by appointment. I have used this gym and trainers for many years. For the past three years I have been taking LaBarre classes at Studios Etc., 110 N County Road and I can't begin to tell you how good this exercise makes me feel. My body is more toned, my posture and balance have improved and I look and feel much better in my clothes. Owned by Palm Beach locals Lauren Donovan and Jaquelyn Quesada, the studios offer daily group classes and private classes and has a small retail boutique featuring one-of-a-kind clothing and jewelry handpicked by the owners. Studios Etc. define their LaBarre classes as, "A power-packed one hour class that tones your arms, sculpts your abs and lifts your tush. It is a blend of ballet, yoga and pilates beneficial for all ages." For additional information visit www.studiosetc.com.

Recently two ladies (photo page 28) went through a total "NEW YOU" makeover in my total makeover program. Their results were amazing. In addition to new hair and clothing styles, they toned their bodies by taking the LaBarre classes at Studios Etc. Here is their testimony: Reina (black cocktail outfit) said, "La Barre classes strengthened my core so I no longer have continual back issues. It also has made me cognizant of my posture and I am much more flexible which is so important as we age." Judith (white outfit with leopard coat) said, "Anita's 'New You' program was the kick-in-the-pants I needed. I enjoyed the intense exercise of LaBarre and the new hair styling from Frank Cassi Beauty Salon, but I am most pleased with loosing 20+ pounds. I found that this one-year comprehensive program did a much better job at encouraging and assisting me to make a true lifestyle change. It was a great experience plus I made new friends." In addition to loosing weight, each lady also lost significant inches from their bust, waist and hips.

For more information about how you can take part in the "New You" program email anitagabler@womenandfashion.net.

beauty essential secrets

Cleansing and moisturizing your skin will help keep your skin supple and smooth. Remember to always treat your face, neck and décolleté as one. I can remember my mother saying to me when I was a little girl, "always take good care of your skin and when you apply your creams always apply them in an upward motion." My mother's skin was beautiful.

Always remove your makeup with a cleansing lotion before you go to bed and never use soap because it is drying. Fighting wrinkles is a challenge. To help combat wrinkles always use sunscreen, drink lots of water and get plenty of sleep. Consult your dermatologist for specific prescriptions such as Retin A.

New products are always coming on the market. For more specific information on what products work, I recommend the book by Andrea Robinson titled, "Toss the Gloss, beauty tips, tricks and truths for Women over 50+." Andrea has been a guest speaker for my Women and Fashion luncheons and she is a wealth of information on the subject of skin care.

Saks Fifth Avenue and Neiman Marcus on Worth Avenue have experienced makeup artists. I especially recommend Maria Propst, a representative for Laura Mercier at Neiman Marcus and Dori Mazer, a representative for Giorgio Armani at Saks. They are always helpful with choosing the right makeup products and makeup applications.

I am a firm believer that as we age, less is best. Here are my bare essential makeup secrets (always test products first and read warning labels). The bare necessities that you should never leave home without. Depending on where you are going, decide how much makeup you need. As a rule, always use sunscreen for daytime followed by primer, tinted moisturizer and a little color on the lips. A more finished look is created when moisturizer, primer, foundation, eye liner, eye cream, under eye concealer, mascara and lip and cheek color are used.

Some of my favorite products include the following items.

MOISTURIZERS

Avalon Organics with Vitamin C Cleansing Milk - Use this for makeup removal and the **Intense Defense Renewal Cream with Vitamin C** for night. This moisturizer really does help smooth fine lines and wrinkles. I especially like the fresh orange scent. Both can be purchased at Whole Foods. For an all over body moisturizer I love the **Olay Complete** all day moisturizer with broad spectrum SPF 15. It is light in texture and great for sensitive skin. **Natural coconut oil** is another exceptional moisturizer. It gives your skin a fresh youthful look.

Laura Mercier Tinted Moisturizer - This product is a tinted moisturizer with SPF 20 and comes in oil-free and regular. It's a lightweight formula that moisturizes the skin.

PRIMERS AND PERFECTERS

Giorgio Armani - Skin Defense Primer with Broad Spectrum SPF 50 - Apply this primer after your moisturizer has dried. This product prepares your skin for the foundation, makes your skin smooth and it has a fresh clean scent. It really is an amazing product!

Laura Mercier Primer - Apply this as an invisible layer preparing your skin for makeup. It makes your skin super smooth.

Garnier BB Cream 5-in-1 Miracle Skin Perfector - It has broad spectrum SPF 15 sunscreen and comes in a few shades. I use the light/medium shade. Be sure to follow the directions on the tube if you plan to be out in the sun for a long time. This product gives the face a healthy glow. I usually receive compliments when I use this product.

FOUNDATIONS

Giorgio Armani - Luminous Silk Foundation - I have been using this foundation for more than 6 years. It is fabulous! It covers dark spots, redness and evens out skin tone. Put one squirt on a makeup brush and apply evenly over your face and blend under chin area. Carefully match the correct color to your skin tone. The Giorgio Armani makeup counter at Saks on Worth Avenue will graciously help you with this.

EYE CREAM

One of my favorites is **Giorgio Armani Crema Nera Eye Cream.** It brightens and targets wrinkles and puffiness while illuminating and hydrating. It can also be used over your makeup to refresh and reactivate. Apply this product with your ring finger, patting gently under the eye and orbital bone.

Laura Mercier Flawless Skin Eyedration Moisture Eye Creme is another favorite. It is a soothing formula that hydrates and increases the skin's ability to retain moisture to help minimize the early signs of aging. This luxurious buttery creme formula hydrates, nourishes and soothes the delicate eye area. Immediately eyes look refreshed, renewed, awakened and less lined. I really like the smooth silky finished look that it gives your under eye area.

CONCEALERS

Cinema Secrets Pro Cosmetics - Light Blue Neutralizer - This concealer hides dark circles under the eyes and dark spots on your face. Take a thin makeup brush and apply a very small amount under the eyes and on any areas with dark spots on your face and blend. If your under eye area seems dry, apply a hint of eye cream first or mix it in with the concealer. I discovered this product a few years ago when I was having my makeup professionally done and it is now a must-have in my makeup bag. You can order it online by emailing donnakelly@mac.com.

EYE ENHANCERS

Eyelids - Lining the eye is important because it frames and highlights the eye. The **Giorgio Armani pencil** has a smudge tip at the opposite end of the pencil plus the pencil goes on easily.

Eyebrows - Having perfectly shaped eyebrows is like an instant face lift. Have them professionally done by someone you trust. A good alternative to waxing and tweezing is threading. It is especially good if you have sensitive skin. Threading is an art and should be performed by a trained professional. Threading creates clean lines and helps slow hair regrowth. If brows need to be filled in, **Giorgio Armani** makes a high precision brow pencil that provides a natural hair look and is easy to use. A trick that I use to make my brows stay in place is to spray hairspray on a brow brush and then brush them in an upward and slightly over motion. Your brows will look perfectly manicured all day.

Eye Lashes - First curl your eyelashes. Heat your eyelash curler with a blow dryer. CAUTION - before you curl your lashes, touch the curler to be sure it not too hot. You do not want to burn yourself. Once the temperature is comfortable, curl your lashes and you will be amazed at how large and shaped they become. Now apply your mascara. Start from the bottom of the lash upward. Only apply one or two times to the top lashes. That way there is no chance of it running during the day.

Here are my favorites.

Laura Mercier - Full Blown Volume Supreme Lash Building - it gives lashes a thicker, longer and natural feathery appearance.

Cover Girl Clump Crusher by Lash Blast - this gives the lashes a thicker, longer and natural feathery appearance. I especially like the curved brush applicator.

The Lancome Bi-Facil Double Action - Eye Makeup Remover - is the best! It is gentle for sensitive eyes and even removes waterproof eye makeup.

BLUSH AND TINTS

Cream or powder blush is a personal preference. It is essential to make your face come alive. **Nars** makes a 3-in-one cream that can also be used as lipstick, blush and eye shadow. My favorite color is a natural peachy shade called Orgasm. There are many colors to choose from. Pick the one that looks best on you. If you have large pores, I recommend a powder blush. **Laura Mercier** makes many shades of blush and is an excellent product. The key to blush is to have it appear as a subtle accent on your cheek bones.

Giorgio Armani - Fluid Sheer #2 - I apply a small amount over my face after my makeup is on. This product gives a slight glow to the skin. Do not over do it as a little goes a long way.

LIP PRODUCTS

Lipstick and Lip Liner - Red lipstick is my favorite but it is important to choose a shade of red that best suits your skin tone. The same red can look totally different on different people. I think **Chanel** makes a great product. I love #440 Arthur, Rouge Coco Ultra hydrating Lip Color. It has a hint of coral in it. Try different reds to see what works best for you.

Nars is another company that makes quality products. I especially like my namesake, "Anita." It is a neutral shade that goes with any outfit.

Laura Mercier makes a soft coral creme lip color that I absolutely adore called "Palm Beach." Again, choose what best suits your skin tone. As for making lipstick last, I suggest applying a thin layer of foundation on your lips first and applying the foundation above the lips helps minimize lines. Use the same makeup sponge or brush that you used to apply the foundation on your face to apply to your lips.

Another tip for masking fine lines above the lip is to line your lips with the clear lip pencil made by Laura Mercier prior to applying your lipstick. The pencil helps prevent lipstick from bleeding. Also try using **RéVive Lip Perioral Renewal Serum** for vertical lines both day and night. Be sure to follow the application instructions. If you use a lip liner, match it as close to your lip color as possible. This will help make your lips look fuller.

Chanel Lip Gloss - Intense Radiance Lip Gloss - Choose a color that best flatters your skin tone. One of my favorites is #165 as it looks great by itself or over a matte lipstick.

Lip Maximizer - Dior Addict Lip Maximizer - This is a definite must-have for luscious full lips. It has an incredible volume effect immediately when applied. Its' unique collagen enriched formula leaves your lips looking plumped up in an instant. I love the tingling feeling on your lips as it makes you feel that it is really doing its job.

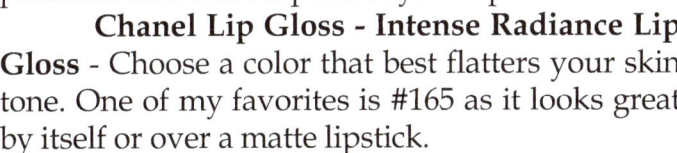

"Beauty is not generic, quite often,
the thing that makes you memorable
is the thing that makes you different."
~ Laura Mercier

MAKEUP BRUSHES AND SPONGES

These tools are essential for applying makeup flawlessly. **Laura Mercier** makes quality brushes for every eye, cheek and lip application.

There are many more types available but here are the ones that are essential. Starting from the top right are brushes that must be in your makeup wardrobe - **Cheek Color** for blending, **Concealer** under and around eyes, **Smudge** for adding depth close to the lash, **Flat Eye Liner** for applying exact placement of color along the lash line, **Angled Eye Colour** designed for an overall application and contouring the crease area, **Pony Tail Brush** for blending eye shadow. Not shown, but essential, is a **Lip Colour Brush** which allows for precise lining of the lip line. Be sure to clean your brushes often!

This one-of-a-kind egg shape sponge ensures flawless application of any complexion product, cream blush and more.

Go to **www.beautyblender.com** for more details. I absolutely think this sponge is amazing. It really does work. I purchased mine at Neiman Marcus on Worth Avenue.

"Make-up is the last thing to enhance your beauty, but it's very important because it builds up your self- confidence and gives you more courage."

~ Evelyn Lauder

HAIR BRUSHES

The **Mason Pearson** hair brush hand-made in London, England is in a class by itself. Invented by Mason Pearson in 1885 it is described as a "pneumatic rubber cushion hair brush." I especially like the one made of 100% boar bristles (bristles are gathered without harming the animal). It gives your hair a clean, glossy and healthy appearance. These brushes come in two sizes. I prefer the small because it fits perfectly in my purse but if you have lots of long hair, get the big one. Saks Fifth Avenue on Worth Avenue carries this product and you can also get in on Amazon.com.

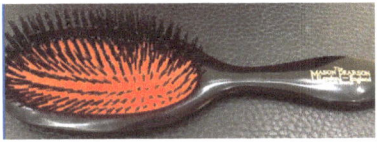 

SKIN PERFECTING

These two products really work. NOTE: I do not use them on the same day. Alternate one or the other every other day.

Dr. Dennis Gross - alpha beta daily peel - A two step, daily peel formulated by Dr. Gross featuring a unique blend of 7 alpha & beta acids is designed to give skin a radiant youthful appearance. This product makes your face peel so I only use it two or three times a week.

Laura Mercier - Flawless Skin Face Polish - I use this product about twice a week in the shower. It is a creamy scrub with purifying microbeads that cleanse and exfoliate. I always make sure that I include my neck and chest area in the process. Place a small amount onto your fingertips and gently massage into the dampened skin. Rinse with warm water. If I have a little extra polish, I rub the tops of my hands with it. It keeps your face and hands smooth.

PERFUME

THE SCENT OF A WOMAN - HOW DO YOU WANT TO BE REMEMBERED? Coco Chanel was once asked where one should wear perfume and her response was wherever one wishes to be kissed. She also said that when you leave a jacket behind, it should be recognized as belonging to you because of its scent. Raymond Matts, a fragrance expert and guest speaker at one of my Women and Fashion luncheons was asked where to spray perfume so it will last. His suggestion was to spray it at the nape of the hairline. I have followed his suggestion ever since.

Perfume is a personal preference and the same perfume can smell differently on different people. My advice is choose what you like but never wear too much. If you receive compliments on your perfume, stick with it.

My favorites include the following scents:

Hermès - Merveilles - It reminds me of my travels to France and makes me feel elegant. I receive compliments on this fragrance.

Hermès - L'Ambre Des Merveilles - It has a hint of vanilla. I wear this for more casual outings and have also been complimented.

Chanel No 5 Eau Premiere - My Mother, who I adored, wore Chanel No 5 when I was growing up but I find the original scent a little overpowering. I enjoy the updated version that was created in 2007, and I recall beautiful memories of my mother when I wear it.

"A woman's perfume tells more about her than her handwriting."
~ *Christian Dior*

GYMS, HAIR SALONS AND SPAS ON THE ISLAND

There are so many wonderful gyms, hair salons and spas on the Island that it is hard to choose just one. I have been to most of them and here are my preferences.

STUDIOS AND GYMS

Studios Etc., 110 N County Rd (561-833-9393) offering Barre, Cycle, and Pilates.

Palm Beach Fitness, 165 Chilean Avenue (561-655-5554) has a full service gym.

SALONS

Frank Cassi Beauty, 125 Worth Avenue (561-833-7883) is where I have been going to colorist Maria Arias and stylist Edwin Rivera for several years. I am always pleased with their work. Owner, Cassi Frielich, is an expert colorist and trained Maria so you will be happy with either of them. In season, make your appointment in advance since this exclusive salon is very popular.

Deborah Koepper Beauty, 215 Sunset Avenue (561-833-656) is a full service salon and the owner Deborah also specializes in skin care and makeup.

Other Island salons and spas:

- **Colorist Hair Studio & Spa (Aveda)**,150 Worth Avenue, Suite 213 (561-659-4055)
- **Frederric Fekkai**, 301 Australian Avenue (in the Brazilian Court Hotel) (561-833-9930)
- **Le Bazaar Palm Beach**, 333 S County Rd (561-345-3770)
- **Shibui Palm Beach**,138 N County Rd (561-822-5450)
- **Spa Cara**, 283 Royal Poinciana Way (561-868-7010)
- **The Spa at the Breakers**, One S County Rd (561-653-6656)
- **The Spa at the Four Seasons**, 2800 S Ocean Boulevard (561-533-3715), 2842 S Ocean Boulevard (561-540-6440)

Valentino

3

Island Shopping Secrets

There are a multitude of wonderful shops on the Island that bring fashion and accessories from all over the world to Palm Beach. The following stores are some of my favorites.

DEPARTMENT STORES

These luxury department stores showcase famous designers from all over the world such as Carolina Herrera, Tory Burch, Etro, Dolce & Gabbana and Prada. They also represent many makeup and skin care lines. Personal shoppers are readily available to assist you.

Neiman Marcus, 151 Worth Avenue (561-805-6150) www.neimanmarcus.com

Saks Fifth Avenue, 172 Worth Avenue (561-833-2551) www.saksfifthavenue.com

DESIGNER BOUTIQUES

Emilio Pucci, 150 Worth Avenue, Suite 109 (561-655-7070) www.emiliopucci.com

During the 1950's Emilio Pucci began designing his signature prints with graphic, geometric patterns and joyful colors.

The clothing, made in Italy, is made of stretch silk and is weightless, unlined and wrinkle-proof (travel friendly). Accessories including fabulous scarves, shoes and bags are also featured.

Akris, 150 Worth Avenue (561-839-1830) www.akris.com

Based in Switzerland with 90 years of experience, this boutique just moved to its new location in Palm Beach. The clothes and accessories are beautifully made and an item I particularly like is the Ai bag, a trapezoid shaped bag designed by creative director Albert Kriemler.

You can create your own Ai bag by choosing the colors for the leather, closure, handle and, if you wish, you can personalize it with your 3 initials. This bag has three convertible looks: rectangular shopper, pure trapezoid tote or signature tote with turn lock, clamp pocket and detachable zip pouch.

Chanel, 301 Worth Avenue (561-655-1550) www.chanel.com

Pearls, tweed fashions, costume jewelry, black dresses, quilted handbags, two-toned shoes and designer perfume were initially created and made famous by the quintessential fashion designer of the 20th century, Coco Chanel.

She believed cascades of pearls framed and brightened the face and made a black dress look devine. Her two-toned shoes had a purpose. The black toe shortened the foot and the neutral tone on the rest of the shoe lengthened the leg.

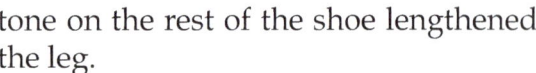

Her handbag with quilted leather was said to be an indication of her love of riding as a young woman. The chain served as a shoulder strap - golden metal plaited with a leather cord - suggestive of horse bridle harnesses as well as belts

worn by the Catholic nuns who educated her as a child. If you are looking for a classic Chanel pump or the latest Chanel bag or fashions, the friendly Worth Avenue staff is always willing to help you find exactly what your are searching for.

Salvatore Feragamo, 200 Worth Avenue
(561-659-0602) www.ferragamo.com

This store was founded by Salvatore Ferragamo, in the early 1900's, who dedicated his life to the search for a secret - the shoe that fits well. When he began studying human anatomy in the United States he found his first clue to the problem being the distribution of the body's  weight over the joints of the foot. He wrote, "I discovered that the weight of our bodies when we are standing erect drops straight down on the arch of the foot. I constructed my  revolutionary lasts, which support the arch, make the foot act like an inverted pendulum."

 Initially noted for its beautiful shoes, this boutique carries elegant sandals, dresses, sweaters and fine leather goods.

Valentino, 204 Worth Avenue (561-659-7533)
Many Valentino fashions are marked by his signature butterfly and the clothes and accessories are exquisitely made.

"I love the 2000's because everyone started to love haute couture."

~ Valentino

Max Mara, 216 Worth Avenue (561-832-0069) www.us.maxmara.com

Originally noted for impeccably made coats and jackets, this boutique now carries many fashion-forward pieces of clothing, shoes and bags.

SPECIALTY SHOPS

Altona, 150 Worth Avenue (561-832-0303) www.altona.com

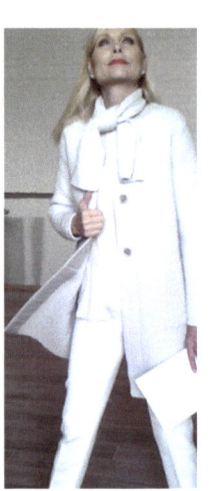

Owner Caroline Freese began her career in fashion more than 30 years ago as a sweater designer in Paris. She opened her store in Palm Beach more than 19 years ago and specializes in casual chic clothing. Caroline carries the wonderful slacks pictured to the right, that are made in Germany called "Seductive." They come in a variety of colors and fabrics, are slenderizing and make a great travel piece.

Match at The Breakers Hotel, One S County Rd (561-659-8469) www.thebreakers.com

Match is one of my favorite shoe stores on the Island! The salon is the ultimate resort shoe boutique offering a unique mix of flats, sandals, wedges, espadrilles and high heels.

" I did not have three thousand pairs of shoes. I had one thousand and sixty."

~ Imelda Marcos

Flowers of Worth Avenue, 205 Worth Avenue (561-514-0660) www.flowersofworth.net

Owner Faith Murray with her Fine Arts Degree is super creative in her use of color, form, texture and design. Both Faith and her staff have expertise in the care of plants and orchids. In addition to everyday occasions such as birthdays, anniversaries and holiday florals, they provide arrangements for private homes, yachts, dinner parties and corporate events.

Kate Spade, 225 Worth Avenue (561-366-1384) www.katespade.com

The Palm Beach store features the "Madison Avenue Collection," a collection only carried in three of its stores in the US. Novelty bags and a large collection of shoes are also a must-shop-here experience.

"All it takes are a few simple outfits. And there is one secret: The Simpler The Better."

~ Cary Grant

Bibi's Boutique, 250 Worth Avenue (561-833-1973) www.shoppbibi.com

Nothing like the best for your pet! Catherine Louis, owner, opened her shop in 2005 and in 2014 expanded to a larger space right around the corner. This custom canine couture shop carries beautiful collars, harnesses and leashes made of quality leather or canvas in a variety of colors and prints. The shop also carries dog beds, books and accessories.

Letarte, 311 A Worth Avenue (561-659-0897)
www.latarteswimwear.com

Often featured in Sports Illustrated magazine, this boutique carries unique swimwear and beach-to-street fashions.

Two sisters, Lisa and Michele Letarte, opened their flagship store in the year 2000 in Maui, Hawaii and currently have eight boutiques in the US.

The "skull" print is their signature design displayed in every collection.

Tourneau, 175 Worth Avenue (561-832-8812) www.tourneau.com

This store with new and pre-owned luxury watches offering prompt service and repairs including battery replacement is the place to go for watches. The staff is always so pleasant!

Il Papiro, 347 Worth Avenue (561-833-5696) www.ilpapirofirenz.com

In Palm Beach since 1994, you can experience a taste of Italy with fine writing papers, journals and lovely handmade decorative papers. If you are looking for special place cards, pens and unique ink this is the place. The owners John Leon Celleri and Marilyn Rivera are always there to help answers your questions.

Spring Flowers, 320 Worth Avenue
(561-832-0131) www.springflowers.com

Inspired by European fashion for children, Maria Flieger opened her first shop in 1993, with 4 now in the U.S. Her goal was to put together a "well-heeled" children's wardrobe. Her shop provides everything from casual wear, underwear, infant layettes, socks, coats and dresses to spectacular pieces for special events such as weddings and black tie galas. The smock dresses and hooded sweaters are my favorites! As for the company's name, Mrs. Flieger looked to her, then three, very young children for inspiration. "Children are just like spring flowers. They're full of life, beautiful and put a smile on our faces. My children are my spring flowers." Now her three children are adults and help her run the business.

Eyes On The Island, 209 Royal Poinciana Way
(561-802-6266) www.eyesontheisland.net

The Eyes On The Island team is eager to serve you including Dr. Herbert Simkin, the Island's only licensed optometrist, Ben Endler, L.D.O., office and optical manager and pleasant efficient staff members. High quality services and advice are provided to all patients.

Luisa Spagnoli, 309 Worth Avenue
(561-557-4069) www.luisaspagnoli.com

This store, new to Worth avenue in 2016, is one of two in the United States and was founded by Luisa Spagnoli in 1928 in Perugia, Italy. Now the third generation designs dresses, slacks, sweaters, blouses and accessories. The fabrics and styles are absolutely devine and one of my favorite stores in Palm Beach!

Maria Saverino, director for Luisa Spagnoli, is always available to help you make that perfect fashion selection.

Mildred Hoit, 265 Sunrise Avenue
(561-833-6010) www.mildredhoit.com

This boutique specializes in classic and contemporary fashion and gifts. I especially like her Magic Coat. Made of parachute silk, the trim and lining are genuine fox and weigh less than 1lb., coat is reversible, the collar is detachable, has been tested to withstand 20 degree fahrenheit weather and comes with it's own travel pouch. This coat is a travel must-have! Another interesting item and a great gift for the woman who has everything is her Handbag Raincoat. This cover fits most bag sizes, has an adjusting velcro and comes with its' own travel pouch.

Sparkle Shoes and Shoe Repair, 243 Sunrise Avenue (561-832-7455)

This store is the best when it comes to making worn shoes look like new. Using a red rubber material, they do an amazing job on red soles for Louboutin shoes.

It is recommended by the owner, Victor, that you take your shoes to be soled before you wear them for a longer life.

PB Boys Club, 307 S County Road (561-832-9335)

If you surf, skateboard, snorkel, paddleboard or skimboard then this is the shop for you. The Wentley family opened their business 29 years ago featuring equipment, beach attire and lessons for the preppy Palm Beacher.

Aristokids, 309a S County Road (561-832-3596)

Next door to and owned by the same family as PB Boys Club, Jodi and Rick Wentley, this store sells comfortable casual clothing for the entire family.

Susan E. Riley, 240 Worth Avenue (561-315-7828)

Celebrating her 23rd year as a designer, Susan E. Riley is tucked away in the enchanting Worth Avenue courtyard Via Amore. Known as "The Princess of Lace," Susan specializes in couture for weddings, rehearsal dinners and special soireés.

Her magical mix of imagination, design and tailoring, combine to create a deftly designed collection, beautifully constructed with silk linings, French seams and bound buttonholes.

Susan also carries a sporty collection called The Palm Beach Yachting Company, featuring both romantic and carefree clothes for yachting and jetsetter lifestyle.

Lori Jayne Monogramming, 301 S County Rd (561-514-9199)

Lori Jayne Bernstein began her career at 9 years old making barrettes covered in unique fabrics.

Seventeen years ago Lori opened her own shop in Palm Beach where she specializes in on-site monogramming for personal and gift items.

A few years ago she opened a second shop at 304 S County Road (561-855-4290), specializing in luxury items such as fine linens, pillows and gift items and on-site engraving customized to your specification.

She can put together all kinds of fabulous one-of-a-kind gift bags for weddings, showers and parties. Lori is a delight to know and her shops are a real treat!

"When I first moved to New York and I was broke, sometimes I would buy Vogue instead of dinner. I felt it fed me better."

~ Carrie Bradshaw

OUTSTANDING RESALE SHOPS

Fashionista Palm Beach, 296 S County Rd (561-249-6302)

This luxury retail and resale boutique is owned and managed by Monique Javarone. The shop features both sophisticated European and American classics.

The Church Mouse, 378 S County Rd (561-659-2154)

This high-end resale shop is owned and operated by volunteers from the Church of Bethesda-by-the-Sea. Proceeds benefit local charities. The clothing, accessories, household items, linens and home furnishings are mostly donated by local island residents and often are rare finds!

Classic Collections, 118 N County Road (561-833-3633)

Sally Kimball owns and operates this high-end consignment shop showcasing clothing, handbags, accessories, costume jewelry and fine jewelry for women.

Classic Collections Gentry, 114 N County Road, (561-619-9307)

Also owned and operated by Sally Kimball, this shop is for the "discerning gentlemen" and offers formal wear, designer shoes and ties, fine jewelry, antiques, artwork, luxury home decor and gifts. Some items are new, where others are pre-owned or on consignment.

"The difference between styles and fashion is quality."

~ Giorgio Armani

Lobster Salad, Cafe L'Europe, Palm Beach, Florida

4

Fashionable Dining in Palm Beach

B*uon Appetito!* Much of the Palm Beach lifestyle revolves around fine dining. The Island hosts a plethora of elegant restaurants serving American, Continental, Asian, French, Italian, Seafood and more. In season (November to March) all of the restaurants require reservations. Evening valet parking is available at most of them.

Here are some of my favorite spots on the Island:

AMERICAN / CONTINENTAL

Cafe L'Europe, 331 S County Rd (561-655-4020) www.cafeleurope.com

Continental cuisine at its best prepared by master chef Norbert Goldner and served in three elegant settings: brasserie, dining room and wine room. Specialties: beautiful flowers, piano music, lobster salad (pictured left), seafood linguine, porterhouse veal chop and osso buco. This is truly a special occasion must. Dinner: Wednesday - Sunday. Prices: expensive.

The Colony Hotel, 155 Hammon Avenue (561-655-5430) www.thecolonypalmbeach.com

With three unique dining experiences, this hotel has a choice for all palates. For music lovers, the Polo Steak and Seafood restaurant features live music to enjoy over a fabulous steak, including the always popular Motown Friday Nights for dancing.

At Café 155 one can enjoy a light New York deli style breakfast or lunch.

The Palm Court offers breakfast and lunch al fresco and prepares great party set-ups as well. Dining poolside is my favorite especially when I'm in the mood for a great hot dog. After eating, walk through the hotel's beautiful herb garden.

Buccan, 350 S County Road (561-833-3450) www.buccanpalmbeach.com

Elegant but casual style, lively bar scene, beautiful people and high ambient energy make Buccan an Island "scene."  Specialties: Tapas/small plates include steak tartare, ricotta ravioli with lobster, mushroom pizza, cheesesteak sliders. Large plates include steak frites, seared sea scallops, extensive wine list, excellent service. Clay Conley, one of my favorites, is the creative chef. Dinner only, open 7 days. Prices: moderate.

Chef Clay Conley

Bricktop's, 375 S County Road (561-855-2030) www.bricktops.com

A Palm Beach favorite, popular for lunch and dinner. Comfortable inside and patio dining. Specialties: The Palm Beach Crab Salad is outstanding. Also offering small plates, seafood, cheeseburgers, steaks, and chicken. Open 7 days. Prices: moderate.

Leopard Lounge, (located in the Chesterfield Hotel) 363 Cocoanut Row (561-659-5800) www.chesterfieldpb.com

Jet black lacquered walls, (picture page 55) window blinds and leather banquette seating are complimented by a leopard skin patterned carpet. The menu features an eclectic mix of classic American, English, Oriental and International dishes.

Guests can also enjoy al fresco dining in the courtyard or by the pool. An afternoon tea is available. Breakfast, lunch and dinner. Prices: moderate to expensive.

Leopard Lounge, Chesterfield Hotel, Palm Beach, Florida

Cucina, 257 Royal Poinciana Way (561-855-7799) www.cucinapalmbeach.com

"Mediterranean island chic decor", family friendly restaurant. Open daily from 10am - 3am, for lunch, Sunday brunch, dinner and their legendary night life. The eclectic American cuisine includes fresh seafood with a raw bar, homemade pasta, Neapolitan thin crust pizza with vegan and gluten free options. Charming spot especially if you are lucky to get an outside table. Prices: moderate.

Palm Beach Grill, 340 Royal Poinciana Way (561-835-1077) www.palmbeachgrill.com

Always crowded with a noisy, lively and engaging bar scene. Outstanding food at reasonable prices, beautiful people, ambient energy, reserve wine list and impeccable service. Reservations are a must. Specialties: grilled artichokes, crab cakes, Ahi tuna burger, NY strip steak, sumptuous hot fudge sundae. Despite the noise, a personal favorite. No corkage charge but will not accept opened wines so don't decant. Prices: moderate to expensive.

Honor Bar, 340 Royal Poinciana Way (561-209-2799) www.honorbar.com

Small in size but big in spirit, drop by sharable snacks and delectable sandwiches. Both the Palm Beach Grill and the Honor Bar are part of the Hillstone Restaurant Group, a first rate run organization.

Taboo, 221 Worth Avenue (561-835-3500)
www.taboorestaurant.com

A Palm Beach landmark and a personal favorite. Active bar scene that often includes visiting local celebrities. Specialties: Continental-American cuisine, generous drinks, interesting people watching. Lunch and dinner. Prices: moderate.

ASIAN

Echo, 230 Sunrise Avenue (561-802-4222)
www.thebreakers.com

A long serpentine bar accommodates a bustling and lively bar scene. Fueled by good food, good wines, good beers and mood lighting, Echo merits a special visit. Start with complimentary edamame and select from a wide variety of Asian cuisines including

sushi, sashimi, more than twenty specialty rolls, seafood and open flame wok creations. The Echo tempura shrimp roll is outstanding. Prices: moderate to expensive.

Imoto, 350 S County Road (561- 833-5522)
imotopalmbeach.com

Imoto (Little Sister) sits right next to Buccan: innovative Japanese and Asian influenced cuisine. Cozy Izakaya style dining atmosphere, two small bars. Specialties: sushi, sashimi, tuna and foie gras sliders, Kalbi marinated beef and other wood-fired small plate selections. Dinner only. Prices: moderate.

Tuna and Foie Gras Slider

FRENCH

Café Boulud, (located in The Brazilian Court hotel) 301 Australian Avenue (561-655-6060) www.cafeboulud.com

Elegant atmosphere inside or on the courtyard terrace serving breakfast, lunch and dinner. The menu balances signature Boulud dishes and French favorites inspired by Daniel's restaurants around the world, with a spotlight on the region's seafood and produce. Specialties: 3 course Le Prix Fixe, seasonal dishes. Prices: moderate to expensive.

Chez L'Épicier, 288 S. County Road (561-508-7030) www.chezlepicier.com

New to the Palm Beach dining scene but fast making its mark with French - Canadian cuisine and a French country décor. Chef Laurent Godbout has won numerous awards in many international competitions. Prices are moderate to expensive.

Chez Jean-Pierre, 132 N County Road (561-833-1171) www.chezjean-pierre.com

Authentic French bistro cuisine with outstanding specialties: fresh Dover Sole, Veal Milanese, Coq au Vin, roasted Chilean Seabass and chocolate Profiteroles. Always crowded in season with a mix of the Palm Beach old guard.
Extensive wine list featuring 350 selections, predominantly French and American. Prices: expensive.

ITALIAN

Al Fresco, 2345 S Ocean Boulevard (561-273-4130) www.alfrescopb.com

Located at the Par 3 Golf Course on the beach with an outdoor veranda and sweeping views of the ocean, golf course and palm trees. Specialties: good pizzas, hamburgers, excellent service. A must visit for lunch or afternoon drinks. Breakfast, lunch and dinner. Prices: inexpensive to moderate.

Bice, 313 1/2 Worth Avenue (561-835-1600) www.bice-palmbeach.com

Excellent Italian cuisine in tasteful indoor and outdoor settings. You will never be lonely at this lively happy hour bar scene. Specialties: seafood risotto, linguini with clams, good wine list. Lunch and dinner. Prices: moderate to expensive.

Jové Kitchen & Bar, (located in the Four Seasons hotel) 2800 S Ocean Blvd. (561-582-2800) www.joverestaurant.com

Specialties: modern Italian cuisine featuring a variety of innovative pastas by chef Luca Moriconi including Strozzapreti (choke the priest) al Frutti di Mare. There are three dining settings: quaint and cozy indoor, outdoor near the pool and a surreal ocean ambience (until 6 pm) which is as delightful a spot to enjoy a cocktail or glass of wine as any place on earth. Prices: moderate to expensive.

"People who love to eat are always the best people."

~ Julia Child

Pizza Al Fresco, 14 via Mizner (561-832-0032) www.pizzaalfresco.com

Located in the same via as Renato's off Worth Avenue. Specialities: charming outdoor setting, palm trees and moonlight, a variety of outstanding pizzas, pastas and good service.

Children are welcome and well-behaved pets permitted. Highly recommended for a casual night out. Prices: moderate.

Renatos, 87 Via Mizner (561-655-9752) www.renatospalmbeach.com

Elegant ambience with indoor romantic candlelight and outdoor courtyard charm, outstanding food, excellent service, pricey wine list. Specialties: rack of lamb, veal chops, pastas. A favorite of the Palm Beach establishment. Lunch and dinner. Prices: expensive.

Trevini, 290 Sunset Avenue (561-833-3883) www.treviniristorante.com

Charming outdoor courtyard dining in season. A blend of northern and southern Italian cuisine. A personal menu favorite is the lemon sole francese - a world class dish! Lunch and dinner. Prices: moderate to expensive.

Sant Ambroeus, 340 Royal Poinciana Way (561-285-7990)
www.santambroeus.com

The elegant decor was inspired by Gran Caffe's of the 1950's in Italy. Open for breakfast, lunch, afternoon tea and dinner. My personal favorites: the Misticanza Poinciana Salad (bib lettuce with cottage cheese, almonds, and scallions in a light ginger dressing); Orecchiette e Burrata (pasta with broccoli rabe pesto, fresh burrata, peperoncino and Piedmontese toasted hazelnuts). Prices: moderate to expensive.

SEAFOOD

PB Catch Seafood & Raw Bar, 251 Sunrise Avenue (561-655-5558) www.pbcatch.com

Specialities: oysters, clams, shrimp, fresh fish including local pompano and a surprisingly good hamburger. Buy one get one cocktails and raw oysters between 4:30 and 6:30 (specials subject to change). Prices: moderate to expensive.

SMALL PLATES

HMF, (located in The Breakers Hotel) One S County Road (888-273-2537) www.thebreakers.com

Named after Henry Morrison Flagler, lively and stunning venue with a cozy opulence atmosphere, a variety of good food and an eclectic list of wines by the glass. Worth a special visit

for drinks and light dinner fare. Excellent service. Free parking if you have your ticket stamped by the wait staff. Prices: moderate.

STEAK HOUSE

The Flagler Steak House, One S County Rd (561-653-6355) www.thebreakers.com

A charming club-like indoor atmosphere and comfortable outdoor terrace with views overlooking the golf course and the West Palm Beach skyline. Specialties include excellent chargrilled steaks, an extensive wine list includes many by the glass. Lunch & dinner. Prices: Moderate to expensive.

Meat Market, 19 Bradley Place (561-354-9800) www.meatmarket.net

Upscale steakhouse with a Miami modern atmosphere. Separate, hopping bar scene where hot pants are sometimes on display. Avoid the meatloaf and stick with the steaks. Large but pricey wine list. Dinner only. Prices: expensive.

BREAKFAST, LUNCH, DELIS, COFFEE, ICE CREAM and SPECIALITY SHOPS

Piccolo Gelato, 66 Via Mizner (561-832-1705) - homemade gelato of all flavors.

Sandwich Shop at Buccan, 350 S County Rd (561-833-3450) www.buccanpalmbeach.com - Entrance around the corner on Australian, open every day 11:00 to 3:00, carry out.

Greens Luncheonette, 151 N County Rd (561-832-0304) - Located in Green's pharmacy, an old fashion luncheonette open for breakfast and lunch, popular with both local residents and snowbirds.

Sprinkles, 279 Royal Poinciana Way (561-659-1140) www.sprinklespalmbeach.com - Ice cream and sandwich shop, open 7:30 am to 10:00 pm.

BREAKFAST, LUNCH, DELIS, COFFEE, ICE CREAM and SPECIALITY SHOPS - *continued*

Surfside Diner, 314 S County Road (561-659-7495) www.surfsidediner.com - Popular breakfast and lunch spot, open 8:00 am to 3:00 pm.

Starbucks, 150 Worth Avenue (561- 651-7740) - Open 8:00 am to 7:00 pm

Patick Lézé, 229 Sunrise Avenue (561-366-1313) www.patrickleze.com - French bakery and sandwich shop, open Monday to Saturday 7:30 am to 4 pm.

Café Delamar, 326 Peruvian Avenue (325 Via DeMario) (561-659-3174) www.cafedelamar.com - Regular menu with Monday through Saturday specials changing weekly. Breakfast served till 11:00 am. Lunch delivery 11:00 am to 2:30 pm. Season hours Monday to Saturday, 9 am to 3 pm. Great salads and sandwiches.

Too Jay's, 313 Royal Poinciana Way (561-659-7232) www.toojays.com - Full service deli serving breakfast, lunch and dinner, open 8:00 am to 8:00 pm.

Amici Market, 155 N County Rd (561-832-0201) www.myamicimarket.com - Full service gourmet market, catering, deliveries, deli, hot and cold sandwiches made to order, pizza, wine and cheese, open winter Monday to Saturday, 8:00 am to 8:00 pm, open summer Monday to Friday 8:00 am to 7 pm.

Blue Provence, 300 South County Rd (561-249-0522) www.blueprovence.com - A direct source to French cuisine such as Balik salmon, caviar, foie gras, truffles, table settings and home accessories open Monday to Saturday 10:00 am to 5:00 pm.

Island Bee, 261 Royal Poinciana (561-619-3657) www.islandbeepb.com - Vegan cafe, juicery and organic market. open 7:00 am to 6:00 pm daily.

"Ask not what you can do for your country. Ask what's for lunch."
~ Orson Welles

Blue Provence, Palm Beach, Florida

The Breakers Hotel, Palm Beach, Floirda

5

Chic Island Hotels

~

There are large and small, attractive hotels on the Island, each offering a unique ambiance. Listed as follows in alphabetical order.

The Bradley Park Hotel, 280 Sunset Avenue (561-832-7050) www.bradleyparkhotel.com

The entryway is reminiscent of a small European hotel with old world charm. The 32 all-suite rooms have full kitchens and a limited number of well-behaved pet-friendly rooms. Within walking distance of many restaurants and shops.

Brazilian Court, 301 Australian Avenue (561-655-7740) www.thebrazilliancourt.com

An elegant boutique hotel with 80 studios, one, two and three bedroom suites, pool and garden-sunning piazza. Fine dining at Cafe Boulud, hair salon and Frédéric Fekkai spa. Walking distance to the beach and shops on Worth Avenue.

The Breakers, County Rd (877-724- 3188) www.thebreakers.com

A luxurious hotel (pictured left) with beach and ocean views. Modeled after the magnificent Villa Medici in Rome with intricate paintings detailed across the ceilings of the 200-foot-long main lobby and first-floor public rooms. Elegant guests rooms, suites and private Flagler Club suites. Dining facilities include HMF, Flagler Steakhouse, Seafood Bar, Echo, the Italian Restaurant, Circle Brunch and the Beach Club. Two large outdoor pools, a spa and exercise facility are available.

The Chesterfield Palm Beach, 363 Cocoanut Row
(561-659-5800)
www.chesterfield.com

Located in the heart of Palm Beach and two blocks north of world-famous Worth Avenue. Designed in the manner of a European bed and breakfast, the hotel has 53 guest rooms, swimming pool, Leopard Lounge restaurant and bar serving breakfast, lunch and dinner. Al fresco dining available in the cozy courtyard. Pets are welcomed. Charming and intimate.

The Colony Palm Beach, 155 Hammon Avenue
(561-655-5430)
www.thecolonypalmbeach.com

A stone's throw to the ocean and around the corner from the famous Worth Avenue, this small but charming hotel offers rooms, suites and villas. All accommodations have been recently redecorated in bright colors and floral prints. Dine poolside at the Palm Court, inside at the Polo or at Cafe 155 for a light breakfast or lunch. Enjoy an evening of entertainment with famous stars in the Royal Room Cabaret.

> "Fashion is in the sky, in the street, fashion has to do with ideas, the way we live, what is happening."
>
> ~ *Coco Chanel*

The Four Seasons, 2800 S Ocean Boulevard (855-995-9172)
Beachfront elegance with pool, outdoor bar and dining. Select a room with a gorgeous ocean view, relax on the beautiful beach and planned activities for children are some of the great ammenties.

Palm Beach Historic Inn, 365 S County Rd (561-832-4009)
Built in 1923 and originally a general store with rooms and apartments for people who worked in town. Now a cozy inn with 13 rooms, continental breakfast, walking distance to beach and shops, pets are welcomed by Chapman the canine concierge, a 5 year old Golden Retriever and general manager Caitlin Crook.

Anita, Charity Event

summary
Secrets and Pleasures

Each of us are miraculously given life with great opportunities as well as difficult challenges. Only you can make it the best life possible. Life is a process and not always easy, requiring effort and diligent attention to make it successful and fun. I have worked hard at discovering the best way to achieve this for me. I hope my secrets and tips throughout this book can make a difference in your life. Remember, we all need some special guilty pleasures!

tips for a new 'palm beach' you

EDIT YOUR CLOSET
Decide what looks best and what should be eliminated. Then organize according to color and clothing type your blouses, skirts, dresses, slacks and jackets.

UPDATE EXISTING WARDROBE
Choose styles and colors that are flattering to your figure and skin tone.

EXERCISE
Incorporate a routine into your exercise program.

USE SUNSCREEN DAILY
Always apply sunscreen before leaving the house.

PAMPER YOUR SKIN
Exfoliate -Try Laura Mercier Skin Face Polish and Dr. Dennis Gross alpha beta peel two-step treatment.

DRINK MORE WATER
It helps with digestion and losing weight, promotes energy, firms skin, banishes cellulite, reduces stress and flushes out toxins.

MOISTURIZE

Apply your moisturizer to face and body right after you shower. It will lock in moisture.

FOUNDATION

Choose a color that matches your skin tone and try Giorgio Armani Luminous Silk.

MAKEUP APPLICATION

Experience a new makeup application by having your makeup professionally done. I recommend having done with the seasons.

NEW HAIRSTYLE

Consult an experienced colorist and hairstylist for a new look.

CONSULT A STYLE SPECIALIST

If you need some guidance in creating a "New You," please email me anitagabler@womenandfashion.net to schedule a time to discuss your needs and wants. My "New You" program is fun.

You will quickly see results in the way you look and the way you feel.

favorite and guilty pleasures

List Your Favorite and Guilty Pleasures

Listen to your music of choice every day.
> ✓ I love Classical, Big Band and 50's Music.

Exercise routinely and do what you like best.
> ✓ I go to La Barre Class and Palm Beach Fitness.

Never skip breakfast.
> ✓ Mine is usually gluten-free cereal with berries, walnuts and almond milk or oatmeal. Always Hawaiian coffee.

Live by a motto.
> ✓ Every day I try to be thankful, kind and giving to others.

Enjoy special yummy treats but in moderation.
> ✓ Ever so often I splurge with a hot fudge sundae at Palm Beach Grill, a milkshake at Green's Pharmacy or First Growth Bordeaux Wines.

Eat your favorite foods, just control the portions.
> ✓ I can eat any kind of pasta any day of the week.

Explore the world.
> ✓ I love to travel. Italy is my favorite go-to country.

> "Be thankful for what you have,
> you'll end up having more.
> If you concentrate on what you don't have,
> you'll never have enough."
> ~ *Oprah Winfrey*

Dear Readers,

      I hope you enjoyed Palm Beach Fashion Secrets and More. I have enjoyed sharing them with you. If you are interested in the makeover program, a fashion presentation for a special group or private club or if you would like to attend one of my fashion luncheons, please email me.

      In addition, if you have any questions or comments about something you read in this book please email me. Thank you.

                                          Fashionably yours,
                                          Anita

                    anitagabler@womenandfashion.net

www.ingramcontent.com/pod-product-compliance
Lightning Source LLC
Chambersburg PA
CBHW042332150426
43194CB00001B/33